Golden Nuggets

Your Guide to Practical Spirituality

MANDY ARWÉN

BALBOA.
PRESS
A DIVISION OF HAY HOUSE

Scripture quotations are taken from the Holy Bible, New Living Translation, copyright ©1996, 2004, 2015 by Tyndale House Foundation. Used by permission of Tyndale House Publishers, Inc., Carol Stream, Illinois 60188. All rights reserved.

Balboa Press books may be ordered through booksellers or by contacting:

Balboa Press
A Division of Hay House
1663 Liberty Drive
Bloomington, IN 47403
www.balboapress.com
1 (877) 407-4847

Because of the dynamic nature of the Internet, any web addresses or links contained in this book may have changed since publication and may no longer be valid. The views expressed in this work are solely those of the author and do not necessarily reflect the views of the publisher, and the publisher hereby disclaims any responsibility for them.

The author of this book does not dispense medical advice or prescribe the use of any technique as a form of treatment for physical, emotional, or medical problems without the advice of a physician, either directly or indirectly. The intent of the author is only to offer information of a general nature to help you in your quest for emotional and spiritual well-being. In the event you use any of the information in this book for yourself, which is your constitutional right, the author and the publisher assume no responsibility for your actions.

Any people depicted in stock imagery provided by Getty Images are models, and such images are being used for illustrative purposes only. Certain stock imagery © Getty Images.

Print information available on the last page.

ISBN: 978-1-9822-1984-0 (sc)
ISBN: 978-1-9822-1986-4 (hc)
ISBN: 978-1-9822-1985-7 (e)

Library of Congress Control Number: 2019900399

Balboa Press rev. date: 01/11/2019

Contents

THE NEXT STEP

Dedication

I lovingly dedicate this book to Charlie,
Ted and Archangel Michael.

To Charlie, my ten-year-old brown and white shih tzu who brought
happiness, joy, playfulness, silliness, strength, and an abundance
of love into our family and household. I miss you every day.

To Ted, my ex-husband turned dear friend. I am so grateful for
your never-ending support of me and my work. You are the best!

To Archangel Michael - this book could not exist without
You. Thank You so much for writing it with me and
Divinely Inspiring me. I love You and I adore You.

Introduction

olden Nuggets – Your Guide to Practical Spirituality is a Divinely Inspired spiritual empowerment book written by Archangel Michael and myself. The chapters include concepts, ideas, and Divine perspectives that I believe in. They are active in my daily life. It is my goal to energize my readers, broaden their perspectives, and encourage them to accommodate the changes that come.

This book is not religious but practical in intent, filled with guidance and wisdom that I have accumulated throughout my spiritual journey, which began in 2004. It is my hope that once you have read a few chapters, you will begin to see with more clarity and with profound understanding. Each chapter begins with a poignant quote meant to develop your thinking about the subject it precedes. The quotes are meaningful to me, and they set the tone for each chapter.

Each of the chapters features guidance and beliefs that I have established through the many workshops, conferences, and lectures I have attended, the classes I have taken, the many books I have read, the spiritual intuitive readings I have given and received, and the online course "Sixth Sensory Training" (a course I took in 2016 that was presented by Sonia Choquette.) The information also comes through my intuition and inner guidance system—my conviction that spirit works with us daily to help us expand and grow.

'Spiritual Wisdom' has been written in order to boost readers' spiritual awareness. 'Expert Living' promotes concepts that can empower you pragmatically. 'The Next Step' gives the reader food for thought on Divine subjects that they may not have thought about in depth.

My wish is for you to welcome the new, update the old, and open yourself to unfamiliar yet important information that attends to your consciousness gently and lovingly. As Will Bowen writes in *To: You Love, God,* "A certain mind is a closed mind. A questioning mind is an open mind." If a concept is uncomfortable for you, consider it, then go on to the next. Apply all that you can. Open your mind and your heart. Phase out old beliefs that no longer serve you.

Finally, after the last chapter, "Guardian Angels," there are two meditations for you to embrace. They are self-loving and broad in scope. They always create a warm and wonderful feeling inside of me when I experience them. I thank you for the light and love you bring into the world, and I wish you the happiest life imaginable.

Blessings to you,

Mandy Arwén

SPIRITUAL WISDOM

Chapter 1

The Power of A Blessing

God doesn't bless us just to make us happy;
He blesses us to make us a blessing.
— Warren W. Wiersbe

The power of a blessing is amazing to observe. When you bless something or someone, you send positive energy to it or them and influence the outcome of a situation in a positive manner. To bless something is to bypass all negative feelings and call upon a Higher Power to influence your outcome.

What is the typical response when something goes awry? Many people curse, criticize, and complain. That very response opens the door for more hardship—it actually attracts it. When you bless the challenging situation or person, you attract a positive outcome. You are actually improving your circumstances and your relationship to the situation or person.

Blessing someone or something is akin to increasing their wellness and wisdom. The more you bless others, have compassion for others, pray for others, and refrain from contributing negatively, the higher your aspirations are. Think of complaining, criticizing, and judging people as withering your aspirations. The idea is to keep your spiritual aspirations high.

Blessing someone or a situation is one of the most effective ways to influence something with positive results. A blessing invites God to Divinely orchestrate the best result for all concerned. The other effective way to have a positive influence on a person or situation is to pray. Remember, when you bless someone, the blessing boomerangs back to you, and you yourself become blessed.

Start by blessing those people and pets that you love and admire. This will create a positive energy flow with them and improve your relationships too. This spiritual practice can be much more difficult when blessing people who have hurt you in some way. But bless those who irritate you or always seem to bring negativity into your life. These are the people and relationships that need to be blessed the most! It won't take anything away from you; in fact, it will raise your aspirations and improve your situation or relationship with that person.

It is so important to realize this—you can absolutely improve your experiences and relationships through the power of a blessing as well as prayer, showing compassion and withholding criticism and judgment. Become a 'blessing expert': try it for a month, and see the miraculous results for yourself. It is spiritual law, there is no question of it working. Bless! Bless! Bless! Make a positive difference in your life and the lives of others.

This is a wonderful way to begin your day:

I bless my family.
I bless my friends.
I bless my coworkers and supervisors.
I bless everyone I will be on the road with.
I bless anyone who has hurt me.
I bless my day.
I bless my food and drink for today.

I bless my car.
I bless my body, mind, and spirit.

This sets up a marvelous day filled with positive energy and the intention that things will go well. The law of attraction says that "like attracts like," therefore the more positive we are about our lives, the more we draw in positive happenings. If anything goes wrong in your day, immediately bypass negative feelings and bless, bless, bless it repeatedly. The effects may surprise you.

Keep raising your aspirations, keep filling the bucket, and watch as conflicted situations turn into harmonious experiences and your life changes for the best. Building up your aspirations is like filling up your own life with blessings. God knows, God pays attention, and God blesses you too.

Years ago I was a junior high school choir and orchestra teacher. The parents of my students were very supportive of me and my program. However, there was one parent who took to calling frequently to complain. She called so often that I dreaded listening to my voice mail. Once I learned about the power of a blessing, I began to bless this parent every morning on my drive to work…and sometimes even once I was in the classroom.

I knew the power of a blessing was powerful, but I was still overwhelmed with surprise when a few days later, this parent called my voice mail and left the friendliest message. She apologized for having been so fussy and said that I was doing a great job. That happened just about a week after I started blessing her. I also began blessing each of my students each day, with wonderful results.

Now I bless people throughout my day. I know that this spiritual practice benefits me, the people, and the world directly. Another example from my life made itself apparent when I encountered rude drivers on the road. I immediately blessed them. Now, I encounter courteous and polite drivers. When I merge, someone always waves for me to go in front of them. My whole driving experience has changed.

It is my pleasure to bless anyone I have contact with: drivers, cashiers, waitresses, and those who seem to be having a tough day. I also bless situations, for example when I witness a car accident or an ambulance going by.

My relationships are much more harmonious, and I don't become aggravated as easily. I feel that I am really doing some good in the world. I encourage you to work with the power of a blessing for yourself and notice the results. Be consistent and persistent. If everyone blessed everyone else, just imagine what kind of world we would live in.

Chapter 2

What is A Blessing?

When I started counting my blessings, my whole life turned around.
— Willie Nelson

Do you ever wonder what actually happens when you bless someone or something? I used to wonder that if by blessing someone I was giving them a 'one-up' on myself. I thought that maybe a blessing meant asking God to favor their situation over mine. Maybe blessing someone was asking God to give them more than I had.

None of these things are true. Not even close.

I have since learned that to bless someone or something is to send them love, protection, God's favor and angels to help them, to make them feel loved, or to do what is most needed at that time. (Angels are our Heavenly Father's messengers and Divine helpers.) As soon as I learned that, I began sending blessings to people all day long. What a great way to have a positive effect on the world!

Now if someone is irritating me, I bless them (silently). Then I intend that God's Heavenly goodness immerse them in love, wisdom and protection.

I normally use my mornings to bless the people I love, one at a time or sometimes in groups. A terrific benefit to blessing someone is that a blessing will come to you too. What goes around comes around. What you sow, you reap. So when you send out a blessing, you yourself become blessed. Keep in mind that "like attracts like," so if you are blessing someone—sending them positive, loving energy— then loving, positive energy comes back to you.

Situations can certainly be improved by blessing someone. On my way to my teaching job, I used to bless each class, every student, every teaching agenda I had for the day, and every instrument in the room. I even prayed for my teaching ability to improve. And everything always was better after blessing all of those people and situations. I now make it my daily habit and joy to bless the people I pass on the road, the gal who serves me my latte at the drive-through, policemen (an excellent idea for several reasons), the bus driver who takes my sons to school, and the kids' teachers. While it might sound arduous, it is truly a pleasure to know that I am sending positive, protective energy to so many people who affect my life and my family.

There is a universal law at work here. When you bless something or someone, it becomes your blessing too. All that you give out comes back to you—so send out positive energy and receive positive energy back. When you are aggravated by someone, you can bless them or criticize them... Which do you want to bounce back to you?

One way to create positive outcomes is to bless

our president;
our country;
Congress;
the Senate;
the government;
the whole world;
our beautiful planet;

your boss and supervisors;
your managers and coworkers;
your colleagues; and
the company you work for.

Just imagine all of those beautiful blessings going out into the world you live in and coming back to you in a positive way.

I believe that the power of a *blessing* is one of the most important spiritual lessons to learn. Please trust and start blessing everything and everyone in your life. Watch miracles happen. You will enjoy this spiritual practice, and you will be a convert forever. God bless you!

Chapter 3

Gratitude

Cultivate the habit of being grateful for every good thing that comes to you, and to give thanks continuously. And because all things have contributed to your advancement, you should include all things in your gratitude.
— Ralph Waldo Emerson

Being thankful and appreciative is one of the most important spiritual and practical lessons. It is a true sign of growth and maturity to be grateful for your blessings rather than distressed about what you feel is wrong or missing in your life.

Saying thank you to someone who gives something to you— whether it is a gift, a favor, or simply their presence in your life— acknowledges their blessing. I know that when someone thanks me for something I have done for them or given to them, it makes me feel even more loving. It creates a desire within me to do more for that person.

Have you ever been good to someone and not been thanked? It makes you feel stale and possibly resentful. It certainly doesn't encourage you to do more for that person. To be thanked and appreciated is like receiving a hug: it feels good, it feels right, and it uplifts you.

I have a friend who is very generous. When we get together for a visit, she often brings me flowers or something lovely. I not only say thank you, but I take the time to write an official thank-you note and mail it to her shortly after our visit. She does the same thing.

I love these notes. She takes the time to personally decorate the cards she sends, and to thank me for the fun and meaningful time we spent together. It's being acknowledged that feels so good. I always put more energy into our visits because of her appreciation. It creates a desire within me to please.

Just like thanking the people in your life is essential, so is thanking the Universe or God for your blessings. The Universe is always looking out for you, and it does more for you each and every day than you can possibly imagine. It is important to appreciate what God gives you: a great relationship, a dear friend, a good job, inspired ideas, a great parking spot, a short line at the grocery store, creativity, just the right book to read, or anything you perceive as good in your life.

Being grateful shifts you into a higher vibration that brings more positivity, more wisdom, and more well-chosen thoughts. Grace flows through your life and attracts more of the things you want. Not only does being grateful say, "I noticed what You did for me," it also changes your own perspective on the troubles you encounter in life. In the midst of problems, being grateful counts.

Years ago, I was going through a dark night of the soul. I was ill, had major financial troubles, lost my rental house, suddenly couldn't feel my intuition, and became distanced from my friends. I was suffering. However, I remembered to thank God that I still had a place to stay; I was safe; my entire family was supportive and loving; I was able to raise my sons with my ex-husband rather than taking turns with them; and we now had four lovely, joyful dogs instead of two each.

It was part of growing up and seeing life through God's eyes. We are blessed even during our struggles. When you step back and take the time to really look, there are so many blessings to appreciate and be grateful for. And the more appreciative you become, the more good you attract—remember, "like attracts like." If you are focused on positive outcomes and blessings, more good will come to you.

Imagine a tube extending from God directly to you. This is your 'tube of blessings'. Now imagine blessings flowing to you easily and effortlessly…many, many blessings from God to you. Now imagine that you are resentful, complaining a lot, negative in your self- talk or with those around you. If this were to be the case – your 'tube of blessings' would constrict…get a crimp in it and hamper the amount of blessings God can send to you.

Now imagine that you are thanking God for all the good in your life. Imagine that every time you notice God's favor and God's blessings in your life you say "thank You" and your 'tube of blessings' expands and even bulges open. Many, many more blessings can flow to you faster and more abundantly. What goes around, comes around. Everything you send out energetically is attracted back to you. Which would you rather attract? More reasons to complain and more reasons to feel resentment, or more reasons to be grateful and appreciative?

A gratitude journal is a helpful tool to become even more grateful. One idea is to purchase a journal and use it only for your gratitude lists. Make lists of your daily blessings and thank anyone who has blessed you. I once learned that you should make a list of all of your blessings…each and every one. Then make a list of each of your challenges. Compare the two lists and notice how your list of blessings and reasons to be appreciative far outweigh the number of challenges and struggles you are facing.

I did this exercise once and listed 187 blessings in my life…things I was grateful for. My list of challenges was 9. When you look at it this way…isn't it amazing? Express appreciation to God for your blessings. Another idea is to be grateful and appreciative for someone or something you have never been grateful for before. Extend your reach each time. When you see just how many blessings you have each day, it becomes easier to cope with the tough times. Count your blessings throughout each day.

Chapter 4

Declarations of Intent

Every thought we think is creating our future.
– Louise Hay

Affirmations can be crucial when we are engaging in personal and spiritual growth. The way you speak can be considered an ongoing affirmation...a *declaration of intent*. We need to change our thinking habits in order to change our lives. Saying the right positive declarations rewires the brain, shaking loose the negative statements, beliefs, and feelings it held in the past. In order to create positive changes in ourselves, we must retrain our brains.

One of the most important spiritual practices is to affirm what you intend to become. Transformational Speaker Lisa Nichols says, "You are the designer of your destiny; you are the author of your story." Speak well of yourself and to thank God for helping you become it.

I never really loved myself until a few years ago. I was very hard on myself, judged my mistakes very harshly, became easily ashamed, and had low self-esteem. Once I learned about the positive effect of affirmations, I decided to grow and tried declarations of intent with vigor.

I couldn't say them aloud at first. It felt too silly. Instead I wrote them down hundreds of times while saying them in my head. I'd write, "I love myself! I am awesome! I accept myself! I am wonderful!" I did this hundreds of times while watching TV or sitting in the living room with my family. I was determined.

Finally I gathered the courage to say them in my car on the way to work. Wow! That had a magnificent effect on me. I'd say with enthusiasm, "I am confident! I am charming, amazing, and wonderful! I am competent! I am capable! I am enthusiastic! I am dynamic! I am an excellent speaker! I am articulate! I am intelligent!" What a difference these daily voicings made in my life, especially in my teaching demeanor. I became more energetic, well-spoken, happier, more engaged, and more effective.

My confidence grew, and my voice became more influential. After just a few days, I started believing the very things I was declaring. My self-esteem grew, and I became creative with the declarations, making up new ones on the spot. I began to feel great on the inside, where it counts the most. It all came through me—through my inner self. I thank God and my declarations for this transformation.

You can view declarations of intent, or spoken beliefs and desires, as tools to update your old beliefs. When you are stuck on a damaging belief, like the one that says you are not good enough or that you are unlovable, we tend to attract situations that prove us right. One way to break that pattern is to re-align your beliefs, thoughts, and actions by speaking intentions and desires that correct our beliefs about ourselves, that say we *are* lovable, that we *are* good enough, and that we *are* wonderful.

Declarations are most effective when you feel the essence of truth within each one. You rewire your brain and body cells to introduce happier, more powerful thought streams as opposed to the negative streams that keep our blessings at bay and keep us stuck in old patterns.

I believe that our thinking can create grooves: patterns that automatically direct us to the same beliefs over and over again.

When you make effective declarations repeatedly, you can create new grooves that encourage new and more positive thoughts. Your cells will respond to the affirmations and change along with the new beliefs.

There is a right way to make up your affirmations. First, make them about the things you want to bring into your life. Second, keep them simple. Third, start each affirmation with the words *I am*. Some good examples are

I am confident.
I am capable.
I am lovable.
I am healthy.
I am beautiful.
I am smart and intelligent.

The Universe responds to these new words, new thoughts, and new feelings. I live with my ex-husband and our twenty-two-year-old son. The house is actually my ex-husband's house, but we have shared it since 2007. A few years ago I felt that the home my ex-husband and I lived in was lovely but not in good condition. The inside needed to be painted, and we needed a new laundry room and vertical blinds in the living room. I pined for these things for years. Problem was, it wasn't my house. So the one who had to want it was my ex-husband, and he didn't. He felt that it was too much money and just didn't need to be done.

I decided to affirm what I wanted in general terms by repeating to myself, "I live in a clean and elegant home." Much to my surprise, one day he said to me, "We need a new laundry room... I'll call some people and schedule it." I was shocked and appreciative. A few weeks later he said, "I think we should paint the walls upstairs... They could really use it." And that got done. Then he complained that the hot, direct sunlight came brightly through our living room window and decided it was time to get blinds. So he did. Then as a final surprise, he said, "Why don't we have air conditioning installed?" Now that was a miracle for me—I don't like the house to be warm or hot.

I had long requested all of these things, but the answer was always no. Now he was coming up with the ideas as if they hadn't been mentioned before...all after I'd repeated to myself, "I live in a clean and elegant home."

The Universe does respond to the vibrations that we emit—negative statements are affirmations as well. When you say, "I'll never get this right," or "I hate this job," the Universe responds to those statements with more of the same vibrations. Whatever you say and feel—good or bad—will bring forth similar results. It's important to keep your self-talk and conversations positive, uplifting, and advantageous. You'll get what you have been focusing on with your words, feelings, and thoughts. Be sure you say what it is that you want, and avoid complaints or depressing streams of thought.

When I stated these new beliefs about myself, I was changing *me* from the inside. I was becoming a new individual. I was creating 'me' the way I wanted to be, and I saw myself becoming according to a vision I held about myself. I used words like *confident, successful, empowered, strong, healthy, wise, intelligent, loving, compassionate, forgiving,* and *capable*. Hold a clear vision for yourself and say declarations aloud. Make them into a real experience and have fun with them. It changed my life!

As Oprah says, "The greatest discovery of all time is that a person can change his future by merely changing his attitude."

Notice what I was affirming, desiring and believing. I wasn't affirming that ten thousand dollars would arrive by noon, or that I would grow blonde hair naturally. I was affirming new qualities for myself. I was changing beliefs about myself so that my self-esteem would rise and I could grow into the person I wanted to be. I was changing what could be changed: me. My insides, my self-esteem, my inner strength, my inner convictions, my zeal to achieve, and my enthusiasm and passion for life. I wasn't telling God what to do, I was telling *me* what to do. I was inviting myself to grow and become an empowered person. And I was thanking God all the way for working with me.

You are breathing life into your beliefs and desires by stating them aloud with enthusiasm. So avoid complaining and negative declarations.

How many of us wish to attract beliefs like this?

I always get stuck in traffic

It always rains on my day off.

The line I pick is always the slowest.

If you find that you are a complainer, play a game with yourself. For two weeks, try affirming *only* the good in every situation. Each time you catch yourself complaining, just claim a 'do-over' and restate a more positive belief. Re-declare your intention, and choose to believe that something better is happening in your life. See how it goes. But there's one catch: you have to believe your statements. You can't scoff at them and expect miraculous changes to come. You always have a choice.

1. Listen. Listen to what you typically say.
2. Decide. Decide which beliefs you want to upgrade.
3. Create. Make up declarations of intent to say and believe regularly.
4. Do-over. When you make a mistake, simply say "do-over" and restate your new belief in positive terms.
5. Be genuine. Keep it realistic.
6. Be consistent.
7. Always thank God for all the good that manifests through your declarations.
8. Avoid complaining. Or else you might get what you are affirming.
9. Declare your new beliefs aloud. It is more effective and believable.
10. Don't give up. Your old beliefs have been there for a long time. Give your new statements a fair chance to come alive within you.

Good luck, and God bless you!

Chapter 5

Forgiveness

Forgiveness has nothing to do with absolving a criminal
of his crime. It has everything to do with relieving oneself
of the burden of being a victim—letting go of the pain
and transforming oneself from victim to survivor.
— C. R. Strahan

Many people find forgiveness to be the most challenging of spiritual activities. Some people feel that to forgive requires admitting fault, conceding that the other person is right, or apologizing. Please understand that forgiveness is the key to healing oneself. Forgiveness is never about right and wrong. It is about release.

To forgive literally means to give forth—and what you give forth is your anger, resentment, and pain. Withholding forgiveness for too long can actually make you ill. It can breed resentment, ruin relationships, keep you from being heart-centered, and make you miserable. Forgiveness is not only something you do for yourself and your peace of mind. It is also something you do for the other person(s) involved. It is your agreement with yourself to move beyond the pain and into freedom, grace, and self-love. It is also a powerful act of kindness, love, compassion and acceptance toward another.

If someone harms you or a loved one, in order to heal your suffering, you must agree to let go of the pain, let go of the resentment, and release all of the negative energy stored inside of you. If you remember that everyone is doing the best they can given their model of the world and what they have assimilated so far, it is easier to let go of the anger and move into forgiveness. I recommend doing the release meditation at the end of this book.

Several years ago—after going through my divorce—I moved back in with my ex-husband (platonically). As is natural with all divorces, I still harbored resentment. It made things uncomfortable and unpleasant. Once I learned the importance and benefits of forgiveness, and the drawbacks of not forgiving, I began my work diligently. I recollected the things I was stressed about. I did my forgiveness silently, and daily.

Then I blessed him with love every day and asked God to help me forgive. A most wonderful thing happened. I started forgiving him in my heart and came to have gratitude for so many things—for the generous things he'd done for me, for his character, for his devotion to our two sons, for his sweet and caring nature. Once I truly began to forgive, the gratitude came easily. God set things in motion and made it easier than if I had not prayed.

Forgiveness starts with *you*, not the other person, although forgiveness can improve the quality of your relationship and move you into your heart center. (The soulful, spirited, loving part of you resides there). You cannot control what other people do, but you can protect yourself from further pain. If you simply are not ready to forgive—if it's just not an option yet—consider praying for help: "Dear God, please forgive (name) for me and through me. I can't do it yet. Thank You so much, Amen."

Then bless the person over and over throughout each day, silently wishing them health, happiness, and abundance. Wish for the person everything they wish for themselves. Each of these actions softens your heart, making it all the easier to forgive.

Asking God for help is a powerful healing tool that allows you to grow by leaps and bounds. You empower yourself. Remember that the act of not forgiving stores negativity within you. And like attracts like. What goes around comes around. You reap what you sow. What kind of experiences do you want to attract?

If you remain in a state of unforgiveness, it is possible that one day someone will not forgive you. That's one of the best reasons of all to forgive.

Chapter 6

Seeing Through God's Eyes

*God's dream is that you and I and all of us will
realize that we are family, that we are made for
togetherness, for goodness, and for compassion.*
– Desmond Tutu

Each of us would like to be seen in our best light. We wish for others to have compassion for us, to be understanding, to avoid judgment, and to see our most admirable qualities. Do we view others in that way?

It is so important to keep in mind that not all souls have had the same experiences. There are people who are in need of emotional healing from childhood or who have come into this life incapacitated emotionally, and each of us has been through struggles that left us hurting, some more dramatically than others.

When you are tempted to judge someone, take off your 'judgment glasses' and see through God's Eyes. God loves each of us and knows no judgment at all. We are *all* God's children. He is completely inclusive, so we should be too. When you find yourself being critical of someone—maybe because they are so different from you—take a moment to remember that they aren't 'done' yet. They still have growing to do. Their journey is ongoing, just like yours is. As Joel Osteen says, "Where they are – is not where they will be. Avoid judging. If you walked in their shoes, you would be compassionate. We are not here to criticize—we are here to give love to one another."

Some people become aggravated because they feel that the people around them aren't trying hard enough, or don't know enough. But each and every one of us is doing the best we can with the tools we have been given, no matter how our best is perceived by others. Acceptance is key. Leave behind criticism, condemnation and judgment – accept (not tolerate, accept) people's difficulties and differences for your sake and theirs.

To practice compassion, look through God's Eyes. If you're angry or hurt by someone, pray to see them through God's Eyes and enjoy a new perspective. God can see the whole picture, and He sees that we are learning our lessons as best we can.

You'll have much more compassion for others, and hopefully yourself, if you view other people through God's Eyes. While it's easy to criticize or complain about someone who irritates you, it shows utmost growth to take the high road.

You can change your heart from judgment to understanding in a heartbeat. It's a habit. This new habit will increase your compassion for others and eliminate judgment. When I see through God's Eyes, I don't become easily aggravated or annoyed. My relationships are gentler and more harmonious. I don't react to people's behaviors like I used to. I assume the best about the people around me and soften my heart. It is a calm, refreshing, supportive approach that truly makes for a more harmonious life.

This doesn't excuse other people from bad behavior. But it does give us a way to deal with it more effectively. Seeing through God's Eyes means that you see the big picture instead of focusing on flaws.

Can you walk in someone else's shoes for a few moments and see why they act as they do? Can you shift gears and send that person healing light and love—and a blessing too? Try it. It feels great!

Chapter 7

Prayer

*If the only prayer you ever say in your entire
life is thank you, it will be enough.*
– Meister Eckhart

L et me entice you about prayer and praying. Praying can be relaxing, enjoyable, soothing, and relieving. Praying is basically our way of connecting with God more openly and deeply, having faith that He can work with you and through you, guiding you to make healthier choices in your life and working miracles.

Prayer is Divine communication. You are speaking to God, God is listening. You can tell God anything; it is privacy and communion all at once. God will not judge you for all that you tell Him. God listens and prays along with you. He knows exactly what you desire even before you ask. He understands you and wants what is best for you.

Sometimes when I pray, I feel God offering a change of words that will better suit the situation and draw the best results. I always appreciate these new wordings. I have a new prayer journal. I call it my Prayer Keeper. I write my prayers inside, one per page, just a short summary. When a prayer is answered, I place a check mark on the page. I want to appreciate just how many prayers are answered. I don't want to miss out on a chance to show gratitude to God for listening to, enhancing, and answering my prayers. You could say that my Prayer Keeper is also a gratitude journal.

Prayer is the best way to receive Divine intervention as needed. When you are praying, you might consider asking God for the highest good of all concerned or the 'win-win' solution for all concerned. This is a powerful kind of prayer. It shows God that you are considering each person involved and want each person to be Divinely nurtured. It is a method of praying that I try to use all of the time. Thankfully, everyone is accounted for.

I pray throughout my day. I might say (silently),

Dear God,

Please protect everyone on my prayer list today. Please send healing love to Bob and Carol today. Please help my sons do well at work today and keep them safe. Please help me be brave enough to call my friend and apologize for being such a brat the other day. I ask for the highest good of all concerned. Thank You!

Amen.

A prayer list is a great idea. List everyone you care about and want to pray for regularly, and pray, "Please protect and send love to each person on my prayer list."

In dire times, I might pray like this:

Dear God,

I am feeling totally overwhelmed right now. I really need your comfort. Please comfort me and send me

relief. I pray for serenity and peace of mind. I ask for
my highest good. Thank You for all that you do for me.
I am appreciative of You. Amen.

Yet another way to pray is by using declarations:

Dear God,

I thank You for each of my blessings, and I know that I
walk in your favor at this moment. Nothing is impossible
with God, therefore my situation is not impossible to
heal. I have faith that the highest good of all concerned
and the win-win solution are on their way. Thank You
for placing me in the palm of Your comforting hand
and keeping me safe. I have faith that my healing is
imminent and that all is well by Divine design.

Amen.

I believe that what God wants is for each of us to be comfortable with Him; for us to bring Him into our daily lives for the little as well as the big things. I do not believe that God is interested in formalities. He is our Heavenly Father.

One of my favorite prayers is this beautiful praise in times of need. I was terribly sick and miserable. I was in bed fussing about my condition, when I was suddenly urged to stop and turn the conversation around to that of appreciation and gratitude. So even though I was in the throes of suffering, I began my new prayer:

Thank You Lord, for your goodness...
Thank You Lord, for your many kindnesses...
Thank You Lord, for your many mercies...
Thank You Lord, for your compassion...
Thank You Lord, for your never-ending support of me...
Thank You Lord, for my strength...

Thank You Lord, for my vitality…
Thank You Lord, for my increasing and improving health…
Thank You Lord, for your love…

After praying this prayer of praise several times while I was in bed, a few hours later I am convinced that my symptoms faded away and I was well enough to get up and spend time with my family, after being out of commission for several prior days. I am very fond of my new favorite prayer.

Several weeks ago, I was in communication with God in what I felt was a prayer. Once I finished, I had the overwhelming feeling that during communication with God we can mistake complaining to God for actually praying to God. I had the erroneous idea that speaking with God was automatically considered prayer. Then I thought about what I had just said to Him, and realized that I was fussing and not praying. Complaining is negative affirmation…and God already knows what is bothering us, before we even start to explain everything to Him. You might consider praying with hope, expectancy, trust and optimism in your heart.

My first prayer ever was very gruff. It was twelve years ago, and I remember the moment it happened. I was going through a separation from my husband and everything was miserable. I was confused and scared, and worst of all, I did not believe in God yet.

I was about to take a shower, my emotions made my body hurt, and I was at my wit's end. I heard a very soft, gentle, loving voice say to me, "Why don't you pray?" I was stunned. I didn't believe in God, so why would I pray? But there is nothing like desperation to turn a situation around. So I brusquely said, "Okay, God. If You are really there, help me…I can't take this anymore." And a miracle happened. A wave of peace washed over me, in and through my body, and it was physical as well as emotional. Suddenly I was left with a strong feeling that everything would work out, a feeling of peace in mind, body, and soul.

It was a miracle. God really came through for me. I've been praying ever since, although much more lovingly. And He was right.

Things did work out, and I was in a better emotional space to handle the details.

A wonderful way to pray could be to say, "This or something better, please."

This is where you acknowledge that God sees and knows so much more than you do—the whole picture. You are giving God permission to upgrade your prayer. Such a prayer requires an enormous amount of trust.

I have been praying for a car...a nice one that is out of my price range. So I have used a terrific addition to my prayer by saying, "at a price I can easily afford." (Louise Hay's books and movies taught me that.) God found me the right car for the right price – one which I love and was better than all the other cars I was looking at. And it didn't happen until I prayed "This or something better God. Thank You!".

Another great prayer for anyone who is interested in spiritual and personal growth is the Self-Ascension Prayer: "Dear God, I am here, I am open, I am ready! Guide me. Amen." Then sit quietly for several moments and feel what God wants you to know. You may get a feeling or a word, or maybe you will get your response later in the day. It's a prayer that really allows God to intervene and communicate with you.

And please, respond to your answered prayers with a heartfelt *thank You* to God and the Universe for coming through for you. Being thanked always makes you want to do more for someone else.

Chapter 8

Self-Love

You yourself, as much as anybody in the entire universe, deserve your love and affection.
– Buddha

D o you realize that when a relationship is unbalanced, much of the time it is because there is a lack of self-love? If we don't truly love ourselves, we can't have healthy and balanced relationships, because we have empty places inside of us and try to fill them with the love of others.

If we don't love ourselves, there will be a place inside of us that yearns desperately to be filled. Sometimes we will find a relationship that we think fills in the gap, many times at the expense of discernment. Because we are the only ones who can fill that gap.

When we wind up with someone who is not to our benefit, someone who does not bring out the best in us, much of the time we have compromised because we lack self-love. Without self-love, our personal boundaries, discretion, and power falter. And it is not only romantic love that can suffer. Constant caretaking—'mothering'—of a partner or spouse, the person who is supposed to be our equal, can result from a lack of self-love.

When we lack self-love, our self-image suffers: we often do not see ourselves as empowered, confident, or strong inside. But self-image can be strengthened in several ways.

Declarations of Intent. Power yourself up with soul-talk that supports your goal:

I am lovable, loved, and loving.
I am strong, wise, and confident.
I am capable, competent, and wonderful.
I am empowered.
People always love me.

Perform self-imaging. Close your eyes and imagine yourself as a mature, self-assured, strong, capable, lovable grown-up. See yourself as successful at the many things you do in life. See your image doing the things you most want to do well. Create a self-image that inspires you. Do this often until it starts to feel real.

Attend a self-empowerment workshop. I attended one years ago and walked out of there a very different person with a positive self-image, self-love, wisdom, and self-assurance. It was a priceless experience.

Dress up in the nicest clothes you can find and see yourself as important, special, mature and self-confident. Make sure other people see you dressed in your finest, even on your days off. Upgrade your shoes, do your hair up every day. Present yourself to the world.

Pray. Ask God to help you develop self-love.

Practice filling yourself up with self-love daily. Ask Tara, the angel of unconditional love, to send you love each day. Practice loving yourself first. You can't love others in a healthy manner unless you love yourself. As Dr. Wayne Dyer likes to say, "You can't give away what you don't have." You deserve this love.

Think back to your childhood, to a moment when something or someone made you feel unlovable. Imagine the child that you were, and send them a steady stream of love. Tell this child how magnificent they are and how much you love them. Tell them that you will always be there to support them and that they are safe.

Be proactive when growing your self-love. Enjoy the process and watch the wonderful changes within you. God bless you!

Chapter 9

Healing

My self-healing lies in praying for those who have harmed me.
— Marianne Williamson

Another way to use the power of a blessing is to bless your body, mind, and soul as often as you can. I am clairsentient, so when I bless a part of my body, I can actually feel it tingle and awaken. If you bless your body, it will be appreciative:

I bless my healthy major organs.
I bless my healthy blood, water, and oxygen.
I bless my healthy glands, cells, and molecules.
I bless my healthy bones, bone marrow, and muscles.
I bless my healthy chakras and entire energy system.
I bless my healthy teeth and gums and my voice.
I bless my healthy feet, toes, and toenails.
I bless my healthy hands, fingers, and fingernails.
I bless my healthy brain, mind, and hair.
I bless my healthy eyes, face, and ears.

I bless my healthy heart.
I bless my whole healthy body.
I bless my healthy soul!

This is an excellent routine to repeat as often as you can. It is with repetition that the benefits will come. Make this a part of your day, evening, or both. Address every part of your body.

Health affirmations reinforce blessings. Say these health statements each day, and visualize exactly what each statement will look like when it becomes your reality:

I am healthy, vital, and energetic.
I am healthy, wonderful, and wise.
I am strong and have plenty of stamina.
I have plenty of vitality.
I have plenty of strength.
I am healthy and strong.

Finally, expressing your gratitude to God for your health is also beautiful:

Dear God,
Thank You for my healthy major organs.
Thank You for my healthy blood, water, and oxygen.
Thank You for my healthy glands, cells, and molecules.
Thank You for my healthy bones, bone marrow, and muscles.
Thank You for my healthy chakras and energy system.
Thank You for my healthy teeth and gums and my healthy voice.
Thank You for my healthy feet, toes, and toenails.
Thank You for my healthy brain, mind, and ears.
Thank You for my healthy heart.
Thank You for my healthy legs, arms, hands, fingers, and fingernails.
Thank You for my healthy hair and eyes,
Thank You for my healthy spirit and soul.

Blessings and appreciation are phenomenal spiritual practices. Be grateful and bless everything you can think of. It's a proactive way to improve your life.

Chapter 10

Compassion

True compassion means not only feeling another's pain but also being moved to help relieve it.
– Daniel Goleman

There is a universal law that states that everyone is doing the best they can, given what they have assimilated so far, what their model of the world is, and what they've been given to work with. Learning this absolutely changed my beliefs and gave me the compassion to understand why people—including me—do the things they do.

Would knowing that everyone is doing the best they can with what they have assimilated so far help you view people with more compassion? Would it change the way you view hurtful people? Would it change the way you view 'troublemakers'? Or people of a different socioeconomic group?

Compassion comes from living in our hearts. When we come from our hearts, we come from a place of unconditional love and can therefore be compassionate. Unconditional love means that we don't attach conditions or strings to our love for others or ourselves. It means we avoid judging and criticizing, and just love.

We all want the world to be compassionate with us. We crave it. We even feel we deserve it. Compassion works both ways: if we want compassion, we should be more compassionate with others. The law of attraction—another universal law—states that like attracts like: what we give is what we get back. In other words, if we are compassionate with others, others will be compassionate with us. If we judge other people, we will be judged ourselves.

Compassion suggests maturity. It takes practice at first, but once you substitute unconditional love for judgment, your compassion will come easily and swiftly. Being compassionate removes the need to judge people and situations. Loving and compassionate people will normally remove themselves from situations where those around them are being critical or judgmental. As Joel Osteen says, "Criticism (is) not love –(it is) arrogant. We're not here to criticize, we are here to give love. If you walked in (someone else's) shoes, you would be compassionate. Where they are is not where they *will* be."

Remember to look through God's eyes the next time you are having difficulty with compassion—the next time you are being critical or judgmental of others or yourself. God sees through the eyes of compassion to each one of us. If you need that support, that nudge, just ask to see through the eyes of God. This will bring proper perspective and loving kindness. It will also bring a more accurate assessment of the whole truth. Look at everyone and everything through the eyes of loving kindness and compassion. Everybody deserves this gift. Including you.

We can be so hard on ourselves. We deserve to be loving and kind to ourselves every day. If you can't be loving and nonjudgmental with yourself, how can you be that way with others? Always be kind to yourself. Respect your heart. It's the only way to avoid judging others.

Compassion is a high achievement in the spiritual world. It is attainable and worthy of our efforts. The world will be much more pleasant once everyone learns to be compassionate. It is just a matter of time.

Chapter 11

Grief

Grief is in two parts. The first is loss. The second is remaking life.
— Anne Roiphe

Because we lost our beautiful dog Charlie recently, I want to make a few observations on grief. When he died, I wanted to go back in time to the days when he was healthy and vital. The desire to have him back was persistent. I was stunned that he had passed away and filled with questions about what we should have done differently.

Nothing made the pain go away, and I agonized over the way he suffered before he died, and then the terror of having lost him. Then I had an impulse. I decided to thank Charlie for all he contributed to our family. I had a big gratitude session—just Charlie and me.

I started by thanking him (silently, in my mind) for being our sweet boy. I thanked him for the perfect way he fit into our family. I thanked him for the way he used to drag that stuffed bear around the room during playtime. I thanked him for the 'Charlie Dance' he used to do on his back, entertaining us all. I thanked him for ten extraordinary years together. I continued in this vein for quite some time, thanking him for everything he brought to our family.

It was amazing: after my gratitude session, I began to feel less burdened by his passing. I found that connecting with him in gratitude was something I did for me, but also for him. I let him know just how much I appreciated the gift of his presence. I actually felt physically better.

I had been focused on the emotional turmoil of his suffering and unexpected passing. Suddenly my burden felt lifted. The heavy pain in my heart and body was relieved. Gratitude brought me beyond that. My new focus was on the gift of his presence in the family and in my life personally—on his very essence.

The first thing I did after he passed away was collect beautiful photographs of him and place them on the fireplace mantel. Then I set a large, beautiful candle in the midst of the photos. The family used this as a place to grieve and come to terms with his passing. I would sit in front of my favorite photos with a lit candle and ruminate over his goodness, his physical beauty, and his joyful personality. I found myself touching his picture—his cheeks, where I used to pet him when he was with us.

I also kept some of Charlie's things rather than putting them away, so I have heartfelt memories when I see his favorite bed or leash. Strangely enough, I haven't been able to throw out his medication. It sits on my kitchen counter. I know I will dispose of it soon, but right now I want every reminder of him in view.

My family found it very uplifting to sit together and tell our favorite 'Charlie stories': when Charlie would start barking because he wanted his dinner and we weren't moving fast enough; his forlorn expression when one of our other dogs swiped his favorite 'chewy,' as if to say, "Why would anybody take my chewy when I was enjoying it so much?" It was a favorite family moment.

I don't have an antidote for grief, but I offer these activities as a place to begin the healing process and bring some joy to the sadness and turmoil. When my Mother died last year, my family handled it in much the same way. It helped then, too.

I'm keeping Charlie's spirit and memory with me and striving to appreciate the blessing of his life here with us. The loss will always be a sorrow, but I choose to dwell on the ten wonderful years we all had together. I want the miracle of Charlie's life with us to carry on.

Chapter 12

Beliefs

It's not what you look at that matters, it's what you see.
– Henry David Thoreau

Why do we feel about things the way we do? Why do we often equate our beliefs with the truth, when so many of us see things from a different angle? How do internal 'rights' and 'wrongs' come to be inside of us? And who is right?

I have noticed that many of my beliefs are based on unconscious decisions I made early in life, some based on what my parents and grandparents taught me, some based on my discomforts with the world around me. Most important of all, I have come to realize that my beliefs are not higher truths, but are created.

When I was a younger mother I believed that children who didn't finish every morsel of food on their plate did not deserve dessert. When my guides and angels (spirit helpers who assist us through our awareness) questioned when this belief became my reality, I remembered that my grandparents lived through the Depression, when having enough food was a daily concern for their families. Eating at their home on Sundays reinforced this belief because they took the meal so seriously. On one occasion, my mom made me sit at the dinner table for hours because I wouldn't eat my peas. Once I discovered where this stubborn belief of mine originated...it no longer had any meaning for me. All of a sudden it didn't matter whether the children ate every morsel of food from their plates. I eased up and looked at the big picture. And mealtime became much less stressful and more fun. Everyone was happier when I dismantled my belief. Yet until I was questioned about it, the belief was my truth.

Another belief I held was about prosperity. I am a loyal manifester—I use affirmations, picturing, vision boards, vivid visualizations, faith, prayer, and the angels. However, one area of my life was not manifesting—prosperity! I checked in with my angels and asked why my money situation hadn't improved. After all, not only do I use all of these amazing techniques, but in my heart I do believe that I should be financially abundant.

I was very surprised when my angels pointed out that while my prayer quality was excellent, my self-talk and family talk were not in sync. The angels lovingly told me that every time my children asked for an upgraded video game system, I would say, "Why can't you be happy with what you have already? We bought you a new system just two years ago, and it still works. You need to learn to be satisfied with what you already have." Well...darn!

That is an odd thought for someone who believes they deserve financial abundance and the best of all things. So where did this belief come from? Childhood. When I was young, my grandparents—who were prominent in our lives—talked of running after the coal truck hoping a piece of coal would fall off so their family could have heat that night. They talked about how hard things were financially and how important it was to keep good tabs on their money. They were grateful for a job, and spent money very wisely.

Is it wrong to want the best of all things? Of course not. My children, who are now young adults, have great prosperity consciousness. They want what is best. It is us, the parents, who fret about their constant desire for upgrades; we use the same old boom box for fifteen years because it still works, while the younger generation has amazing gadgets and electronic systems that are cool, exciting, and practical.

My belief was to spend money very carefully and make do with what I had. But it was only a belief, not a higher truth. I encourage you to explore your own beliefs and see if any could use some updating. Once the origin of a belief becomes obvious, the belief may no longer seem so indispensable. What was once a hard truth will prompt the question, "Why did I do that?"

Look at what is blocking your flow in life...I bet there is a belief there.

EXPERT LIVING

Chapter **13**

Altars

*I write in my study, where I also have my prayer altar. I believe
that keeps me focused and gives me positive energy and reminds
me that I'm merely the instrument of greater creative forces.*
– Chitra Banerjee Divakaruni

How many of you have an altar in your home? I think altars
are a wonderful way to connect with your spirit. I have four
altars in my home, and spending time with them brings
me delight, inspiration, and sometimes expectation. There are many
reasons to have an altar: to honor a deceased loved one, to have a
sacred place to pray, to cherish your family and spiritual guideposts,
to honor the things that you love and are important to you, to have
a place of beauty, to have a place of serenity, and even just to have a
space of your own.

Your altar is where meaningful items and symbols can be placed.
The more significant the item is to you, the greater the impact the
altar experience will be. It is important to focus on the things that are

meaningful to you. By placing such items on your altar, they remain in front of you, are always visible, become sacred, and create beloved feelings about your altar and your life. You are honoring yourself.

Symbols are meaningful. They can represent the direction of your life. Are you an elegant person? Do you desire more elegance in your life? How about placing a piece of classy ribbon and a sample of high quality perfume or scent on your altar? Are you creative or seeking to be more creative? How about a colored pencil on your altar to represent your creativity? I have a fabric flower on my altar that represents my love of flowers. I love to place fresh flowers on my altar, and when I can't have fresh flowers for a few days, the fabric flower reminds me to buy some more. Do you have a business card? Perhaps place the card on your altar. It can represent your desire for steadier and more reliable business.

My altars are sacred spaces where I keep written prayers; artwork; and symbols of things that I love, that I wish to have, and that represent who I love. My bedroom altar features candles; photos of my loved ones; sage for burning; mandalas that I created on my own; healing crystals; fresh flowers; figurines of angels, Jesus, Mother Mary, Kuan Yin, and Maitreya; a laminated photograph of Saint Lorenzo (patron saint of cooks); my prayers; my latest lottery ticket; a deep purple runner to cover the table; and a brand-new keychain that represents the new car and new home I hope to have one day.

A big candle represents my love for God and all things spirit. When I light the candles, I feel like the energy in my room becomes light and magical. It represents to me that God is working on answering my prayers. My altars are a lovely way to honor people, things, and spirit while lending a nice focus to the things I hope to manifest.

It is so much fun to build an altar—especially your first one! You will most likely change it as you grow and evolve. There is no right or wrong way to create your altar. All that matters is that it is your sacred space and that the items on it are important to you. Don't feel that you need to pray at your altar; prayer time is anytime, anywhere.

I have two altars honoring my mom, who passed away in 2015. We were very close and enjoyed each other tremendously. On one altar I have photos of her, a pair of her glasses, some yarn from her knitting bag, and one of many knitted hats that she made for preemie babies.

On my other 'Mom altar,' I have a small amount of her ashes, a clipping of her hair, a bowl with some things that were important to her, and a beautiful stone that she picked up at the beach on a wonderful trip with her good friend, Anne.

When our much-loved dog Charlie died, my family created an altar of photos and candles to keep him alive in our thoughts and hearts each day.

It can be nice to build a themed altar. A prosperity altar might represent money or successes to be. Get creative, keep it personal, and make it all your own. (But if you use candles, use really nice ones—don't skimp.)

An altar's size is unimportant. You can use a small table with just a few items that are sacred to you, or create a large altar with many, many items. I recommend keeping the altar spacious and uncrowded. Give each item its own place to shine. Regarding the sage that I keep on my altar, it is in a safe, fireproof shell. When I light the candles, I also light the sage; it purifies the energy in the room and smells nice.

Enjoy your altar. Spend time on it. Spend time with it. I think you will be delighted!

Chapter 14

We Train People How to Treat Us

Believe in yourself! Have faith in your abilities!
Without a humble but reasonable confidence in your
own powers you cannot be successful or happy.
– Norman Vincent Peale

In relationships, both people are responsible for establishing good boundaries, right from the start. Often people assume that their friend or partner knows what the expectations are in their relationship. This is a mistake.

We train the people in our lives how to treat us with every interaction. It is your job to establish boundaries with others. Don't make your friend, partner, parent, relative, sibling, or stranger guess where you draw the line.

When we set personal boundaries that are healthy and right for us, we tend to have healthy, satisfying relationships. People know how we expect them to interact with us. When we fail to establish personal boundaries, people learn that we don't have any preferences, or that we don't mind being discounted. They don't do this to be awful—they are just following the tone you set.

We normally neglect to set boundaries at the beginning of a new relationship, when it_really counts. We try not to hurt the other person's feelings, we try to be nice and flexible, and we try not to seem rude. Or we assume that others already know what our needs and desires are or that they *should* know what our needs and desires are.

Conjure a personal and self-assuring vision for yourself. Imagine what your ideal relationship looks like, and how you would like to be perceived. Hold on to that vision as you move toward it in reality.

You are a unique, wonderful, lovable being, and your interests, likes, and dislikes are what make you interesting to others. You are the only person who is just like you; if you want relationships that are healthy, strong and satisfying, you must let other people know who you are, right from the start.

By being your true self, you will have a better chance of attracting rewarding relationships with people who have similar core qualities as you. Remember how unique you are! You are interesting to other people.

Having healthy boundaries is your responsibility. It isn't someone else's responsibility. Sometimes people fail to promote their interests out of a desire to be flexible and understanding. But I want to emphasize that this is a mistake. This is crucial—you count. Your feelings count. Your needs count. You are unique, and your likes and dislikes are part of what make you intriguing to other people. Please do not discount yourself. Doing so can make relationships unbalanced or hurtful.

When I was a young adult, I wanted to please everyone. When a friend wanted to go out to eat, I would say, "You pick the place." If a boyfriend wanted to go somewhere and I didn't, I would acquiesce just to avoid making waves. If someone wanted to play a duet, I'd play music I didn't like, just to avoid a squabble, however small it might be.

In the course of my life, I have given away my personal power because of shyness, low self-esteem, and fear of appearing selfish to others. Once I figured out that I was doing this (during a two day self - empowerment workshop), I became a tad angry with myself for giving it all away with my daily interactions and lack of confidence in myself. I was tempted to be angry with those who intimidated me. However, I know in my heart that the responsibilities lay within me.

Even these days, it is not always easy for me to voice my preferences. I work at it daily. It is so important to realize that I count and need to be my true self around people. I should not try to keep others in their comfort zones if it makes me feel weak and nebulous. I encourage you to do the same. Come out of your own comfort zone and be counted. People may be taken back by your sudden self-expression; don't be surprised if you meet some resistance at the beginning. Stay with it. It does get easier as you practice, and I do recommend practicing.

Visualize yourself in conversation with someone and practice expressing yourself honestly. Pray for guidance and inner strength. Ask God where you need to make changes and how to proceed. Write a script of how you would like yourself to interact in a sample conversation. Write down key phrases you might like to express. Self-awareness is your first assignment. Be insightful enough to choose your conversation options rather than be shy and hold back. Make a list of each thing you are afraid of when it comes to being forthright, and then address each fear with prayer and confidence.

Maintain your personal power as if it were a sacred treasure. Be yourself, and train the people in your life to treat you the way you want to be treated. It's a self-respecting way to be counted. If you train others through your actions, you may find that you are more content. And visualize! See yourself as you wish to be. Set the example in your mind and follow through. Mentally practice training people how to treat you. Success will be yours.

God bless you!

Chapter 15

The Win-Win Solution

*If winning or losing is going to define your
life, you're on a rough road.*
– Bud Grant

Have you ever experienced a conundrum where it is impossible to proceed, because not everyone will be pleased? Have you been involved in a conflict where both sides dig in their heels and won't budge? Where both sides are angry and hurt? Where both sides feel they are right, and both sides sit and wait? This is an unproductive scenario. Each side is stuck.

Some pray for an end to the resistance, some pray for the other person to see things their way, and some pray to come out ahead. An extraordinary prayer in situations like these is the 'Win-Win Solution.' I pray for each side to win simultaneously, so that everyone comes out ahead. God has ways of doing this when you ask.

In the Win-Win Solution prayer, I explain the conflict to God and say, "I pray for the win-win solution—the solution where everyone concerned wins. Thank You so much. Amen." Each time I have prayed that way, everything has worked out and everyone has come out happier.

There is no reason to be in a stand-off with someone, to remain angry, or to hold a grudge. Pray and let God handle things His way. It takes a lot of courage to ask for everyone to come out ahead. You don't have to be stubborn, and conflicts don't have to be immoveable or insurmountable—if everyone wins, it means that you will be happier too. Trust the process and allow yourself to see the big picture. No one has to lose when you involve God.

When you use the Win-Win Solution prayer, you are asking to see through God's eyes—to see all concerned individuals through eyes of compassion. You see the bigger picture. With the Win-Win Solution prayer, you are essentially asking God to show you the best way to proceed, and of course to give everyone a win-win.

I have five Win-Win Solution prayers active right now, and I am so eager to see how they turn out. I have total confidence that everyone involved in my prayers will be pleased and feel like a winner. I love this prayer!

One of my Win-Win Solution prayers currently addresses my heartfelt desire to move forty minutes east of here to live in a glorious home on a gorgeous lake. I have held this soulful desire for several months, however I have been too afraid to let my immediate family even know about this desire because I am concerned about what their reaction will be.

I feel that it is a big conundrum. What I want seems unaligned with what they want and need in their lives. I fear they will resent the forty-minute drive to spend time together, I fear they will think me selfish for uprooting the family pups, and I fear we will not be able to remain as close emotionally to one another with me living outside of our neighborhood. This is why I have employed the Win-Win Solution prayer. I gave this concern and problem to God in order to secure the very best results for each of us, and I knew I could trust God to work things out.

Well, as it happens – God changed my mind! In the most loving way possible, I started thinking that my family being close was far more important to me than living on a lake right now, but that doesn't mean that I won't get to live on a lake somewhere nearby in the future when the Divine Time comes along. I decided to stay and as a gift, God had a new apartment built for me right where I was and everything is new and elegant and beautiful! By asking for God's intervention, the Win-Win Solution came about. I changed my own mind - stayed close to family and had a new home built just for me.

A golden nugget of wisdom that spirit gave me recently is proving very helpful. Spirit whispered to me the other day, "If it is right for you, it is right for everyone concerned." This was a big load off my conscience.

Finally, when you ask for a Win-Win Solution, silently bless each person concerned. Sending positive energy to others is always a great idea, but most especially when you have a concern about something. Bless enthusiastically and feel you have done your best in the situation. God bless you!

Chapter 16

Choose the Right Focus

Once you replace negative thoughts with positive ones,
you'll start having positive results.
— Willie Nelson

What you pay most attention to—with your words, thoughts, and emotions—is what you attract into your life. Like attracts like, so gratitude and appreciation attract positivity, while worry and complaining attract negativity. Your words, thoughts and emotions send out a vibration—and this vibration becomes your point of attraction. Your point of attraction is what draws experiences and things to you and into your life. Be careful what you focus on. Be sure it is what you want in your life.

In his book *Win Forever*, Pete Carroll delineates his beliefs about successful football coaching. The two philosophies that stand out the most for me are "practice is everything" and "do things better than you have ever done before." I believe that to become who you want to be, you must first practice. Practice being the person you wish to become. Focus on the attributes you want to portray. Act like the person you wish to become. The second philosophy, "do things better than you have ever done them before," means to strive to be the person you wish to become. Don't leave it to chance. Be the best *you* you have ever been—regularly. These themes may surprise you, but they can be helpful and empowering for us all.

I have a friend who does his share of complaining each day. It's automatic for him. He attracts aggravating situations routinely: long lines at the grocery checkout, slow-moving traffic, slow lines at the post office. It's funny, though… When I go out, the lines are short and traffic is swiftly moving. I do my gratitudes twice a day, and I dwell on my blessings.

It just makes sense that when you complain, fuss, and worry frequently, you attract more reasons to complain, fuss, and worry. I've seen it in action. There are lifelong benefits to saying gratitudes, being appreciative, and sending love and blessings to people throughout your day. Great parking spaces and swift lines at the post office—just for starters—ought to convince you to switch tactics.

In order to attract the very things you desire, it is essential to pour forth joyful and purposeful emotions about those things. For the same reason, avoid dwelling on your troubles, concerns, or momentary defeats. Think about how much emotion goes into frustration, anger, and resentment. Use your power of choice to de-energize frustration and vitalize hope, love, and gratitude.

From your emotions—your point of attraction—you send vibrations out into the Universe. You can purposely pray for prosperity, great health, safety, and a joyful life…or you can unconsciously harp on the misfortunes in your life, complain, or embrace resentment. Either way, your vibrations will attract more of the same.

Speaking affirmations can help keep things positive and flowing. Get yourself a deck of cards with affirmations printed on them or a book of affirmations. Use them every day to speak peaceful, loving, positive, beneficial sentiments about your life. The more you say them, the more strongly you will believe them, and the more you will see the positive effects in your life.

Relationships are also affected by our positive or negative vibrations. If you are struggling with a person you normally complain about, feel frustrated with, or harbor resentment toward, those negative vibes will prolong the problems and perhaps make them worse. Try speaking words of compassion and love, well wishes, and blessings about the person. This has worked for me on numerous occasions, and it feels great to make that amazing shift without even speaking directly to the person.

Be careful what you focus on, and use your power of choice to choose grateful, loving, hopeful, blessed words and emotions. You might be amazed with the results.

Chapter 17

When It's Time to Move On

The only way to do great work is to love what you do.
If you haven't found it yet, keep looking. Don't settle.
– Steve Jobs

If you are no longer able to be happy in your current employment, would you be open to having a job where you could be more content? Perhaps your job was satisfying at the beginning, but now you have grown beyond it and wish for more gratifying work—a job that serves you best. Maybe you have developed new skills and interests that your community would benefit from if you were available to use them.

If you have expressed gratitude (to God and yourself) about your current job—expressed gratitude for having the job, for earning an income through it, and for the people you work with and work for—and you are still dissatisfied, consider asking God for a new job.

God knows what is best for you, what you like most of all, and what would bring you contentment and a good income. Why not pray about this and ask for direction to find a wonderful new position? Never assume that you have to stay in a job you dislike. Regardless of the job market, God sees the big picture and, if you ask Him, can find you a suitable position in any market.

To remind yourself that a good job is on its way, recite this phrase over and over:

I do what I love,
I love what I do,
And I earn an excellent income too!

If we asked someone why they stay at an unpleasant job, their answer might be, "Where else can I go?" "The job market is bad," "I am already over fifty," or "Benefits are hard to come by." I am not suggesting that you quit your job and then start looking. I am suggesting that you start praying and working with gratitude while you are still employed.

If you start this process from a perspective of gratitude and appreciation for your current job, benefits, coworkers, income, supervisors, and location, you will be in a much better position to have prosperous, joyful, satisfying work in your next job. Remember that you are talented, capable, competent, and skilled. There is someone out there looking for all the qualities and talents you possess. Have faith in yourself. Have faith in God.

It is my heartfelt belief that when your heart wants to make a change, it is because change is waiting for you already. If you feel the need for a new job, I believe a new job is waiting for you and is calling you like a beacon. Brush up on your skills and abilities, be thankful for everything you already have, heal any resentments you may have, forgive anyone you need to forgive, and make a list of all the qualities you would like your next job to have—for example happiness, a kind and organized boss, or a short commute.

Have the respect for your current job that you expect to have for your new job. Be the kind of employee who should have a better job. Expect to do well, and you will.

Chapter **18**

Personal Boundaries

I encourage people to remember that 'No' is a complete sentence.
– Gavin de Becker

When we love and respect ourselves, we have naturally good boundaries with other people. We say no when we want to say no, without worrying about how other people might react. When we lack self-love, we have difficulty saying no and offering our viewpoints and opinions.

Our self-love determines who we naturally attract into our lives. When we lack self-love, we naturally attract people who won't consider our feelings at all, or someone who will walk all over us, or someone who will frequently push our buttons. If we don't set good personal boundaries with others, and with ourselves, people will overstep our comfort zone.

I used to say yes and do things I had no desire, time, or energy to do—simply because the thought of saying no sent shivers down my spine and made my stomach feel weak. I got myself into aggravating situations just because the thought of saying "no thanks" was simply too scary for me.

As stated in a previous chapter, if someone asked me where I wanted to go for dinner, I would respond, "Oh, I don't care…you choose." Each and every time. I was afraid of the embarrassment of expressing my viewpoint only to face opposition from my companion. So I let others choose.

Here's the odd thing: I convinced myself that I was doing this to be nice. I didn't know how to draw boundaries with others, so I told myself I was a very flexible person, a nice and kind person. Someone who could get along with anybody, anywhere, anytime. But did that mean that people who could say no or state where they wanted to eat *weren't* nice people? Were they inflexible? Unkind? Of course not. This was simply how I justified my uneasiness.

Now that I have developed self-love, I naturally attract loving, wonderful people into my life. Each of my relationships has dramatically improved because I (lovingly) say what I mean and mean what I say. Now the people in my life are getting to know what I'm all about, because I say yes and no and share my viewpoints with them. I enjoy my time with people more because I let my voice be heard when decisions are being made. I'm much happier and more satisfied, open hearted, and loving due to my own self-love.

Our boundaries help define who we are to the world around us. Self-love determines whether or not we can set decent boundaries with the world. We meet our own needs. Relationships can naturally be healthy between friends, mates, children, and parents. The love must first start from inside of us and radiate outward.

To develop your own self-love, start with some daily affirmations. In other words, tell yourself how terrific you are:

I am wonderful!
I am worthy!
I count!
I have excellent boundaries!
I am fun to be around!

I am a loving person!
I am smart and intelligent
I am essential to God's Plan!
I love being me!
I can say no anytime I want to!

These short sentences will open up your mind and heart to new feelings about yourself, and should ultimately lead to happier interactions with others. Feel free to create your own affirmations based on what you would like to develop in yourself. After saying them often enough, the affirmations will actually rewire your patterns so that these positive statements become your dominant thoughts and feelings. Enjoy your new boundaries!

Chapter 19

Stress

To everything there is a season, and a time
to every activity under heaven.
– Ecclesiastes (Chapter 3, Verse 1, NLT – Red Letter Edition)

Y ou cannot be in your heart center and be stressed at the same time. Stress lowers your spiritual vibration, keeps you from hearing or sensing your intuition, keeps you on edge, and reduces the amount and quality of your peaceful time, quiet time, meditation time, contemplation time, prayer time, and rest and relaxation time.

I used to have a very busy schedule. I worked very hard as a teacher, drove my sons to their activities, was a den mother for my son's Cub Scout group, and ran errands. I seemed to have no time for myself. I was frazzled, stressed, and becoming even more stressed as I realized the predicament I was in. It was like a rollercoaster that never stopped. I was very unhappy.

One day I made the decision to stop: just stop and make myself a top priority. I put it all in God's hands. I prayed for serenity in accordance with my highest good. Do you know what your highest good is? It aligns you with your greatest contentment and joy.

Within a matter of weeks, my schedule started thinning out naturally. Suddenly my sons didn't want to keep doing each and every activity, so we only kept the ones that mattered most. Carpooling came about, which meant less driving for me. My schedule totally shifted, effortlessly and flawlessly. It was all natural.

Now I was able to become peaceful and serene. I focused on my spirituality—which was exactly what I wanted to do. We usually have control over our schedules but are afraid to tell others, "No, I can't do that." We watch our schedules get heftier and heavier, all the while feeling that we have no choice. Then resentment and stress set in.

We can make more time for rest and relaxation if that is important to us. I think mostly that we have forgotten that it is appropriate to rest and relax every day. You will be healthier and happier for it.

When you first look over your schedule, panic can set in. What do I remove? Who am I letting down? Who do I say no to? How will this all play out? I recommend that you turn it all over to God and trust in His wisdom. Say a prayer to be serene and less busy in your daily life, in accordance with your highest good. Let God guide you through the process step by step. You ultimately have the choice of saying yes or no.

Think of all the heart-centered things you will do with less stress in your life: quality family time, rest, perhaps reading or a favorite passion or hobby. Let these become a part of your day again. Whatever you love and enjoy doing you will do more often and enjoy more if you are stress-free and relaxed. Remember to involve God in your plan—He will look out for your highest good and surprise you with terrific results.

THE NEXT STEP

Chapter **20**

The Gift of Intuition

Intuition is seeing with the soul.
– Dean Koontz

The gift of intuition is truly that—a gift. It is God's most significant way to communicate with us.

Have you heard from your intuition lately? How many of us know where it comes from? What *is* intuition? Intuition has been described as a 'hunch,' or as having a 'gut feeling.' Some people say, "My sense is…" while others say, "My vibes are telling me…"

The truth is that God is telling you; your soul is telling you. When your intuition gives you information, God and your soul have just come through for you! Say thank you and be appreciative.

God and your soul are always looking out for you. When you are about to get yourself into a jam, they can step in and give you that funny feeling in your stomach. Or that bad vibe, or that hunch. Sometimes it will be information that you need to have.

I love my intuition and try to follow its guidance every time it speaks to me.

When I was driving as a young adult, I had a sudden flash of understanding: my intuition gave me a 'golden nugget' about my Mother that, in essence, helped me to be more compassionate.

When I was in college, my boyfriend was expected to meet me and he never showed up. I began to fret and worry. Suddenly, my intuition gave me another golden nugget—that he was fine, had miscommunicated a social obligation, and had gone about his business without calling me.

One day I was at a gathering with my friends. One girlfriend was being rude and unpleasant with me, and I was momentarily confused by this behavior. Then a whisper of intuition told me that she had had a fight with her sister earlier in the day and was still feeling angry about it. She didn't even realize that she was acting out. I certainly felt relief that I wasn't causing her bad mood, and it gave me compassion for her.

I appreciated the information in each of those instances, although I didn't exactly know that it was my intuition. I learned about that later. My intuition has always been strong. I have always felt things, or known better ways of doing things. It could be a source of frustration, because my intuition was always correct yet I had to be patient with those who disagreed with me. It was only a matter of following my intuition despite the resistance of those around me.

God and your soul are always a part of you. Wherever you are. They know all about you and where you are headed. They want the very best for you. There is, however, a catch—*you have to notice.* They can give you the vibes and the hunches, but you have free will, and that means that you can dismiss, ignore, or argue with it. The more you dismiss your vibes and hunches, the less sensitive you become to them altogether. One day you might not recognize them at all.

To strengthen your vibes and hunches, pay attention to every one of them. Follow their advice every time. Never second-guess a hunch. Some suggest keeping a little pad of paper with us at all times and writing down every hunch that we get, checking their validity later on. What a great way to establish your intuition's expertise!

Please realize that intuition is usually a quiet sense, rather than a loud voice. If you are waiting for a sign, an utterance or message – you may miss out altogether. Intuition is - in my experience - calm, quiet, gentle and more a whisper of the soul. The best advice I can give on noticing your intuition is to remain open, receptive, believing it is always there, and grateful once it is received.

I tend to say "thank You" after noticing my intuition... acknowledging God and my soul's input and being grateful for the Divine Communication. I feel that saying "thank You" sets me up for even more communication and even more often. Intuition is a gift – so saying "thank You" is appropriate.

When you follow your hunches, you will develop stronger intuition. You will be guided toward a smooth and conveniently flowing life in tune with your senses, God, and your soul. Have faith in your soul and obediently accept its gifts of insight, understanding, and information. Life gets easier when you trust and go with the flow.

Chapter 21

Death and Dying

We are not human beings having a spiritual experience.
We are spiritual beings having a human experience.
– Dr. Wayne Dyer

This is a very sensitive subject, and I would like to state my own beliefs regarding death and dying. I believe that people who cross over at their time of death are actually *safe, happy, peaceful, serene,* and *alive*. There is no death in the grandest scheme of things. People leave their bodies here and go on as spirit through life eternally. You are eternal. Each of us is eternal. Our life here is part of eternity.

People who are in spirit are happy. They meet up with their friends, loved ones, old pets, angels, and God. They are aware of us here on earth. They communicate with us in a variety of ways: by giving us specific thoughts, giving us their scent, causing us to think of them. I even heard of a case where a father left pennies around the house for the daughter to find, reminding her to watch her finances.

I myself am a medium and have had several communications with deceased loved ones. When my mom died, I connected with her and asked what she did in Heaven. Her response was, "I'm always here with you! Why do you keep it so cold in here?" (I had just bought an air conditioner, and I keep the temperature on the cold side.) I could hardly believe she knew I was keeping the room cold. She also communicated that she was very happy where she was.

Then, after we lost our wonderful dog Charlie, leaving us broken up and devastated, I tried to connect with him because I wanted to make sure he was all right. I couldn't, so I asked my mother in Heaven what Charlie was doing. She responded that he was "greeting his fellow dog friends." He was sorry that he left us, but his body gave out, and he was, according to my mother, ecstatic in Heaven. It was such a comfort to know that he was safe and happy.

It is important to remember that we are eternal. We never die in spirit—only our physical bodies die. In Heaven we go on forever with God and the angels. As Norman Vincent Peale once said, "I believe there are two sides to the phenomenon known as death, this side where we live, and the other side where we shall continue to live." Those who make the transition find themselves in Heaven as spirits/souls and can choose to come back to earth again and again, each time living in new circumstances and focusing on different lessons and experiences. They are truly happy to be home in Heaven when they arrive.

If you wish to communicate with a deceased loved one, start talking directly to them, either aloud or in your head. They can hear you. You may receive an audible answer, an essence or feeling, or a comfort. I was sobbing as I communicated with my deceased mother and Charlie, but I suddenly felt a wave of comfort and peace wash over me. That was when Mom said, "Charlie is sending you peace."

I knew it was true. I *felt* it.

You choose to come into this life on Earth. You choose who to experience life with, where you will be born, and the general circumstances of your life, as well as your birthdate and the experiences you wish to have. Your experiences lead to your growth; some can be challenging, and some are joyous.

Since you choose to come into this life, you can also choose to come back with loved ones in another lifetime. And you will be together in Heaven as well. Your loved ones aren't dead—they are very much alive and well, leading full lives in Heaven until they choose to come back to Earth and live a physical life again.

The spirit world is a wonderful place, from what I have gathered from my spiritual-intuitive-medium experiences. Elisabeth Kubler-Ross said, "Death is simply a shedding of the physical body like the butterfly shedding its cocoon. It is a transition to a higher state of consciousness where you continue to perceive, to understand, to laugh and be able to grow." You will naturally be distraught when a loved one crosses over, but don't worry that they are unsafe or unhappy. They are happy, safe, and loving you from where they are. They can hear you call to them and send you comfort and peace. Always pray for them—for their comfort, peace, and highest good. God bless you!

Chapter **22**

Past Lives

What you need to know about the past is that no matter what has happened, it has all worked together to bring you to this very moment. And this is the moment you can choose to make everything new. Right now.
— Ajay SADH

Have you ever looked into your past lives? Have you ever wondered about who you were before coming into this life? Do you believe in past lives? I do. I have seen several of mine during past-life regressions.

I first became interested in past lives when learning about my spirit guides and angels. Spirit guides and angels are Divine helpers who navigate our lives with us. Their role is that of teacher, wise one, and friend. Once I accepted that we all come here with Divine assistance, it was easier to understand how life continues after a person's physical death. During a psychic reading, I gained great insight into my guides and their names and learned how they were helping me. I even learned that one of them had had a past life with me. At that point I realized that I needed to look into past lives more thoroughly.

I read books with case studies of near-death experiences. The writers' stories closely matched each other in all that these people learned during their experiences crossing over into Heaven. I became more and more interested. I looked up local hypnotherapists and past-life regressionists on the Internet, chose one, and made an appointment. I was extremely excited but nervous about what I would hear and see. In a regression, you relax, and your soul shows you clips from your past lives. You can see and hear what is happening. It is fascinating.

From reading case studies, and during my own past-life regressions, I learned that we have all lived here many, many times before. When we 'cross over,' we have the opportunity to review our lives from beginning to end. We see our triumphs, disappointments, lessons learned, and lessons not yet learned. We make the choice to either come back as yet another incredible person, or stay in Heaven and do our work there. The choice is ours...we have free will.

I watched an entertaining movie long ago called *Defending Your Life*. The movie follows two adults who die, go to Heaven and learn how everything in Heaven works. One significant scene shows these individuals using a "past-life viewing machine." They watch several clips from past lives then view their most recent life. The man sees how he has been ruled by fear most of his lives. He hasn't done the things he wanted to do. The woman, on the other hand, sees her acts of bravery during her lives. The film had created in me a strong desire to see, and learn from, my own past lives.

During my own regression, I sat with the hypnotherapist in her studio, in comfortable chairs. She played relaxing, soft music, and took me through a meditation. Finally, I was extremely relaxed yet still awake and aware of everything that was going on. She asked me what life I was viewing, and I described to her what I saw: I was a starving African woman in a village. I had two tiny babies who had just died of starvation because my breast milk had dried up. I was grief-stricken and miserable, and I died shortly after the babies passed.

This vision made complete sense—it had been reflected in my current life. It actually solved a mystery for me. When my sons were born, I couldn't bring myself to breastfeed them; I was vehement about it, yet I never knew why. Now I knew it was because of that terrifying incident in Africa in a past life.

I learned that I also had a past life in Washington State. I was walking through woods in the Cascade Mountains when a tree fell on top of me and mangled my knees. That correlated with why I have had problems with my knees in this lifetime.

Another interesting past lifetime taught me why I have always been repulsed and frightened by fish—dead or alive. I was shown a life where I was a fisherman on a fishing boat; we had an accident, and I was thrown overboard. As I drowned in the sea, I was surrounded by fish and fish debris as I gasped for air. This death really awed me. I have been disgusted by seafood all of my life—I won't even try it. I can't even cope with smelling fish. It always puzzled me until I had this regression.

I believe we can have physical and emotional carry-overs from life to life. Symptoms of our traumas can show themselves as scars, bad habits, unexplained dislikes, and even mysterious fears. Sometimes we agree to marry a certain person in this lifetime because we have married them before and have unfinished business with them. Sometimes our current sons and daughters were our parents in a previous lifetime.

Researching your past lives through a reputable hypnotherapist can lead to more compassion for yourself. Previously unexplained odd behaviors, fears, and scars can be revealed, providing a sort of relief. There are joys to discover as well. I learned about a happy and wonderful life I had in Austria where I played the flute professionally in a fabulous symphony orchestra. Being a gifted musician in this lifetime, that information brought me joy. When I was a young girl, the very first instrument I chose to learn was the flute.

If you are interested in exploring your past, I recommend going to a reputable past-life regressionist and allowing yourself to discover some of these intimate details about yourself. It may take a few sessions to reveal all of the details you want to know, but be patient and enjoy it! Self-discovery is a process.

Chapter 23

Spirit Guides

Your Spirit Guides and Angels will never let you down
as you build a rapport with them. In the end, they
may be the only ones who don't let you down.
– Linda Deir

When we are in Heaven (what many call the Other Side) planning our incarnation here on earth, we are assigned what are called spirit guides. These guides are people who know us well and choose to work with us, teach us, help and assist us. There was a period of time many years ago when I enjoyed getting psychic readings often. I loved learning from these psychic teachers and I wanted to be just like them.

One of the main things I learned during those readings was that we are sent here with Divine assistance. We are each assigned spirit guides (teachers) and they work with us (mostly anonymously) until we discover them and start asking questions. Once I learned about my guides, I talked to them non-stop in order to learn about them and what I should be doing. It was fascinating to me, and all the while I was aware that out of all the people I knew, I was likely the only person who knew about spirit guides. This was distressing. After all, who could I speak to about my spirit guides? I was fascinated and wanted to converse with others about what I was learning, even compare notes with others.

It turned out that the only people I could talk to about guides were the psychics themselves, which made me sign up for appointments all the more frequently. I immersed myself in books on the subject and learned as much as I could.

Spirit guides are loving, lovable, soulful people who guide us along our spiritual path. They help us achieve spiritual growth. They help us stay the course, follow our path, expand, and get to wherever we are headed. They are compassionate and love us unconditionally, both here and on the Other Side.

Spirit guides work with you in many different ways. They can

- make you feel like you need to buy a certain book,
- introduce you to someone with important information for you,
- make you feel like signing up for a particular class that will further your growth, and
- give you the feeling that you need to do something.

While angels have never incarnated, spirit guides have lived a physical life before. They have first-hand experience about the struggles and stresses of being in physical form. They are extremely compassionate about your trials and tribulations.

As for your main guides, you can learn their names and develop a working relationship with them if you desire, although it is not necessary. Your guides will work with you throughout your life regardless of your awareness of them. They've been with you since your birth.

Several spirit guides have been working with me, by my request, for some time now: I requested the assistance of a music guide, yoga guide, cooking guide, and writing guide. I have been a musician since the fifth grade, mainly on the saxophone, and I know that I have a saxophone guide with me who has nourished and nurtured my playing all the way. He practically plays through me. A while ago I began playing the drums, and once I remembered to call upon a drumming guide, my drumming improved greatly, and right away.

My cooking guides help me create the most delicious and wonderful meals for my family. You can call upon any kind of spirit guides; they are eager to come and help you.

It is wonderful and exciting to get to know your guides by name— just ask your guide for their name and sit quietly. Have faith that the name will come to you. After that, talking to your guide can be easy; chat to them inside your mind and know that they are listening. Tell them your plans for the future. Ask for their help in guiding you to the most direct path. This collaborative approach is very useful in furthering your spiritual development. You work with your guides to ease your own way.

Remember: God chose these wonderful beings to watch over you and work with you. From the Other Side you meet, work with, and love your spirit guides, and they love and want to help you. Feel comforted and start communicating with these lovely, supportive, helpful guides.

Chapter 24

Guardian Angels

*One function of the angels is illumination,
and the other function is that of being a guardian.*
– Fulton J. Sheen

Did you know that you have a minimum of two guardian angels and one archangel with you at all times? Did you know that they have been with you since birth and that God chose them for you before you came to earth? Did you also know that God chose them to help you with your life's path?

I first learned of my guardian angels from a wonderful radio show I listened to each morning. On Mondays the Angel Lady would be featured—you could call in and she would tune in to your angels and tell you their names and what their purpose was with you. When I found out about my angels, I beamed all day. I was so proud to have Joseph, Rachel, and Archangel Michael as my own angels. Their purpose fit perfectly with my teaching career, and later when I wrote this book and began giving spiritual intuitive readings to clients.

I have Joseph, the angel of joy, and Rachel, the angel of inspiration, as two of my guardian angels, and Archangel Michael is with me for guidance and protection. When I was a junior high school choir and orchestra teacher, I inspired my students to perform at a very high level. Rachel was with me in the classroom, helping me be an inspiring teacher every day. Joseph helped me be joyous with my students and in life.

Archangel Michael has always guided me and protected my energy as I go about each day. Your guardian angels always connect with your higher purpose. It's all for your benefit. Many people share the same guardian angels, or share one guardian angel. Angels can be many, many places at one time. I have done readings for other people who also had Joseph, the angel of joy as their guardian angel.

It wasn't difficult believing that we each have guardian angels. As soon as I heard the Angel Lady's radio show and heard the excited voices of the callers when they found out their angels' names and gifts, I just felt the truth in it. For me it was knowing that I felt so inspired all the time because of Rachel's gifts to me. The reason I beam with joy is because of Joseph's influence. And the reason I have such good insight is because Archangel Michael is guiding me. Archangel Michael actually started this book with me way back in 2006. We met each day and wrote each chapter in tandem. Archangel Michael also helped me develop my own wisdom card deck to help read for clients. It is still in handwritten form and I don't use the deck currently, but it was a beloved project and I cherish the time he spent with me. It all fits perfectly. And the Angel Lady had no idea who I was when she gave me this information.

Once I started communicating with my angels, I called upon other helpful angels, and they were happy to come and assist. I called upon the angel of music to assist me in the classroom, the angel of love to bring more love into my relationships, even the angel of teaching to help me with agendas and student discipline.

Once I called upon the angels to come into my classroom, the difference was bright and obvious. The choral students sang like angels themselves! The orchestra had a special ethereal quality, even at the junior high school stage. It was uncanny. I loved the angels' help.

Eventually I started tuning into angels regularly and learned which angels were working with the people around me. I began passing messages to those around me from their angels, and it always delighted the person receiving the message. I was deeply satisfied by doing this and decided that I wanted to do it professionally.

The first official spiritual intuitive reading I was asked to give took place in 2006 through a new friend. She asked me to come to her home and give all of her friends their angels' names and messages. I had never met any of her friends, so it was quite exciting. We all sat in her living room, where everyone was ready to take notes, and I went around the room giving each person their angels' names. A message came through for each person as well. It was so much fun.

Angels love and adore you unconditionally. They are with you to help you live your life more comfortably, courageously, joyfully, and safely. They answer every time you call to them, so call on them all day long! They enjoy the moment we first discover their relationship with us and communicate with them. It's a real celebration.

Angels won't interfere with your choices or free will. Angels are wonderful at leading us to our joy and know what makes our hearts take flight. You are not giving away your power by inviting their assistance into your daily life. You are empowering yourself. Angels are experts at showing us what we are overlooking. They are always loving and will always help with compassion. You will never feel ashamed when an angel comes to your side.

Angels are experts at saving us time and stress. When you want help with another person, they often first show you the other person's viewpoint. Angels bring harmony into tense households and bring about forgiveness in a peaceful manner.

There is an angel for every need:

Need more patience? Call on the angel of patience!

Need more happiness? Call on the angel of happiness!

Need to forgive someone? Call on the angel of forgiveness!

Need a boyfriend or girlfriend? Call on the soul mate angel!

When people say that they have just seen an angel, they likely have not seen it with their physical eyes. They have seen it with their opened inner eye. That does not negate the fact that they have seen it.

More often than not, to get our attention, angels will play a song inside our minds with meaningful words, or show us the same words over and over for a period of days (like on a passing truck, billboard, or TV screen). They may also have different people mention the same necessary information, seemingly out of the blue.

What about people who really irritate us? The best thing you can do is send them *legions* of angels. These are the folks who need angels the most. They need healing, not resentment. Always bless them and then send them angels.

Best of all, angels help us feel unconditionally loved, appreciated, and safe. If you wanted to, you could invite Archangel Michael to stand guard outside your house and car to protect them at all times. A great idea is to ask a particular angel to remain in a room of your home at all times, creating a loving atmosphere: the angel of harmony, the angel of love, the angel of relationships, the angel of cooking, the angel of peace, even the angel of happiness.

Please send angels with your children to school for protection and better focus, with your spouse to work, with yourself throughout your day; you can send angels to be with every driver on the road for safer conditions and peace of mind.

Keep the angels of love, peace, and happiness with you at all times and see how calm and loved you feel on a regular basis. God bless you!

Chapter 25

Meditation for Releasing and Allowing

T his is a meditation that really feels great. It's short yet effective as you renew yourself or wind down for the day. Feel free to add your own sentiments to the process as you become familiar with it.

1. Light a lovely candle and play some relaxing music.
2. Sit quietly and calmly.
3. Close your eyes.
4. Take three deep breaths—inhale through your nose, exhale through your mouth.
5. Picture God's glorious white light cloaking your entire being.
6. Picture all negative energy (like anger, resentment, and unforgiveness) releasing from your body.

Now open your eyes and say (silently or aloud),

*I now release all anger from my body and send it to God's light
for healing.*
*I now release all unforgiveness from my body and send it to God's
light for healing.*
*I now release all shame from my body and send it to God's light
for healing.*
*I now release all guilt from my body and send it to God's light for
healing.*
*I now release all resentment from my body and send it to God's
light for healing.*
I now release all bad habits from my life.
I now release all criticism of others from my heart.
I now release all self-criticism from my heart.
I now release all burdens from my life.
I now release all misconceptions from my life.

Then draw in your good by saying,

I now allow God's love for me to envelop my heart.
I now allow myself to feel and be appreciated by everyone I know.
*I now receive unconditional love from the Universe and everyone
I know.*
*I now forgive everyone for anything that ever offended me or
hurt me.*
*The person I really need to forgive the most right now is
_____ . I forgive any offense, harm, or hurt and bless
them with peace.*
I now ask God to heal me completely and generously.
I now receive all the blessings that God has in store for me.

Again picture yourself cloaked in white light:

I affirm that God is the source of my income and supply.

I affirm that I am prosperous and abundant right now.

I see my heart expanding around my whole body and getting bigger and bigger until it is larger than my entire body, larger than my house, larger than the city, larger than the entire world. My heart envelops the entire world. I now fill my heart with love, and I relax.

Take three deep breaths, inhaling through your nose, exhaling through your mouth. Gently open your eyes and bless your day. Bless all the people in your day. Bless your car and your home. Bless your life and say thank You to God for it.

You are now ready for a terrific day! Carry all the goodness from this meditation with you throughout your day. Continue blessing things and people and saying *thank You* as good things happen to you.

Chapter 26

Meditation for Blessing and Healing

his meditation is about blessings, expressing gratitude, and sending love and healing to those in your inner circle and wider world. It is effective in improving your relationships and healing the world. Feel free to add your own sentiments to the process as you become familiar with it:

1. Light a lovely candle and play some relaxing, soft music.
2. Sit quietly and calmly.
3. Close your eyes.
4. Take three deep breaths—inhale through your nose, exhale through your mouth.
5. Picture yourself immersed in God's white light.

Open your eyes, then think or say gently,

I send blessings of love to each of my family members. (Name each one.)
I send blessings of love to each of my dearest friends. (Name each one.)
I send blessings of love to every person that works with me.
I send blessings of love to my bosses and supervisors.
I send blessings of love to each of my acquaintances.
I send blessings of love to my home and my car.
I send blessings of love to my office space.
I send blessings of love to today's food and drink.
I send blessings of love to those who have hurt me.
The person I really need to send a blessing of love to right now is
_____ *.*

Now send healing energy and the energy of peace by saying,

I now send God's healing energy and peace to each of my family members. (Name them.)
I now send God's healing energy and peace to each of my dearest friends. (Name them.)
I now send God's healing energy and peace to every person who works with me.
I now send God's healing energy and peace to my bosses and supervisors.
I now send God's healing energy and peace to each of my acquaintances.
I now send God's healing energy and peace to each person that has hurt me.
The person I really need to send God's healing energy and peace to is _____ *.*

Now let's expand your healing circle:

I now send God's healing energy and peace to everyone who lives in my town.

I now send God's healing energy and peace to everyone who lives in the United States.

I now send God's healing energy and peace to all war-torn areas of the world.

I now send God's healing energy and peace to all who are hurting in my wider world.

I now send God's healing energy and peace to each person who is suffering in this world.

I now send God's healing energy and peace to our beautiful planet earth.

I now send God's healing energy and peace to our Universe.

I now thank God for each of my blessings and experiences.

Take three deep breaths, inhaling through your nose and exhaling through your mouth. Open your eyes and bless your day. Thank God for a great day and for your life. Thank God for the gift of your loved ones' presence in your life. Thank God for protecting you every day. Stay in a mindset of gratitude.

About the Author

Mandy has lived in Edmonds, Washington since 1998.
She moved here to the Pacific Northwest with her
family from Downingtown, Pennsylvania.

Mandy was a band, choir and orchestra director during her 17
years of teaching. In 2003, Mandy began her spiritual education
and in 2006 started giving Spiritual Intuitive readings.

In 2007, she created her own personal Divinely Inspired Oracle
Deck (which she refers to as her Wisdom Cards) with Archangel
Michael guiding her. Archangel Michael also helped her write
this book – *Golden Nuggets – Your Guide to Practical Spirituality.*

Mandy gives private readings from her home office in
Edmonds, Washington in person, or by phone.

SpiritualWellBeing@Aol.com
www.SpiritualWellBeing.net

Made in the USA
San Bernardino, CA
16 February 2019